The Sonoran Desert
by Day and Night

Dot Barlowe

DOVER PUBLICATIONS, INC.
Mineola, New York

INTRODUCTION

Many of us grew up hearing exciting tales about the desert—about the camel caravans, the heat, the sandstorms, and men dying of thirst in the Sahara. We were led to believe that a desert was a barren, lifeless place. However—though some of what we learned is true—there is another kind of desert. In the American Southwest there is a desert that abounds in life. One cannot turn over a small stone without finding some creature hiding there, and as far as the eye can see, varieties of cactus and other amazing plants fill the landscape. Animals large and small make their homes in this desert. They have become adapted over the centuries to 120-degree heat and the excessive dryness of their environment, and they sleep and raise their young in underground nests or in among the cool recesses of rock crevices. Many can live on very little water, or in some cases none at all. The desert plants have adapted as well, storing water from the infrequent rains in their pads or stalks or roots; some have even evolved to survive animal predation by growing sharp spines.

Our great American desert covers a great portion of our Southwest and reaches northward to part of Idaho and Oregon. This book focuses only on the southern part of that great expanse—on what is known as the Sonoran Desert. The Sonoran Desert covers an area of about 120,000 square miles, stretching from southwestern Arizona and southeastern California down into Mexico—including most of Baja California and the western half of the state of Sonora. As you explore this great desert in the following pages, you will find that it is filled with fascinating creatures, sudden encounters, unexpected music, subtle perfumes, and stunning beauty.

Bibliographical Note
The Sonoran Desert by Day and Night is a new work, first published by Dover Publications, Inc., in 2002.

International Standard Book Number
ISBN-13: 978-0-486-42369-2
ISBN-10: 0-486-42369-7

Manufactured in the United States by Courier Corporation
42369705
www.doverpublications.com

To those who have not seen it before, the world that gradually emerges from the quiet darkness of night is an alien landscape. The sky, miraculous in ribbons of gold, brilliant red, turquoise, and purple, forms a luminous backdrop for the giant saguaros that stand guard, their arms reaching upward, over the smaller ground-hugging plants. Here too, the century plants (tall, thin plants in background), the **mesquite** (*Prosopis* spp.—the spraylike

shrubs in the right middle distance), and the huge orderly mass of **organ pipe cactus** (*Stenocereus thurberi*—behind the mesquites), cut exquisite silhouettes against the gold-streaked horizon. As the color slowly changes to a soft aqua and then to a hard, clean cobalt blue, the desert seems almost lifeless in the encroaching heat. In the ecosystem of the Sonoran Desert, activity will not rise to its peak till after nightfall.

With faint grunting and barely audible scraping of tiny hooves, a small band of **collared peccaries** (*Tayassu tajacu*)—or javelina, as the Mexicans call them because of their javelin-pointed fangs—have come to a pool of water left by last night's thunderstorm, in the midst of a saguaro forest, to drink their fill. The peccaries, with their gray and black hair and a yellowish-white band running from shoulder to shoulder, are the first visitors to the rainpool.

North America's only native wild pig is tough and aggressive, and its appearance anywhere is reason enough for other animals to wait their turn. The **antelope jackrabbit** (*Lepus alleni*) under the yellow-flowering creosote bush waits impatiently for the peccaries to be on their way. His grayish brown body with neat white underside lies half-hidden in the hollow (or "form") he has dug in the shade of the bush.

Their black head-plumes bobbing gracefully, several **Gambel's quail** (*Lophortyx californicus*) run to the rainpool and drink. The plume springs from a bright chestnut crown rimmed with white. Beneath the quail's white-rimmed black throat and face, its grayish body sports a large black spot surrounded by soft yellow, low in the center of the breast. The wings are black with white stripes, and its back is olive gray. Since the peccaries have moved off, the pool has become more lively. The quail and jackrabbit soon will be joined by other birds and small mammals. The temporary pool is a dangerous place for the prey animals, but they are ready for momentary flight. The **desert lilies** (*Hesperocallis undulata*) in the foreground are white with a blue-green stripe on the underside of each petal. The **Salome sulphur** butterfly (*Eurema* spp.) has deep-yellow wings edged in brownish black.

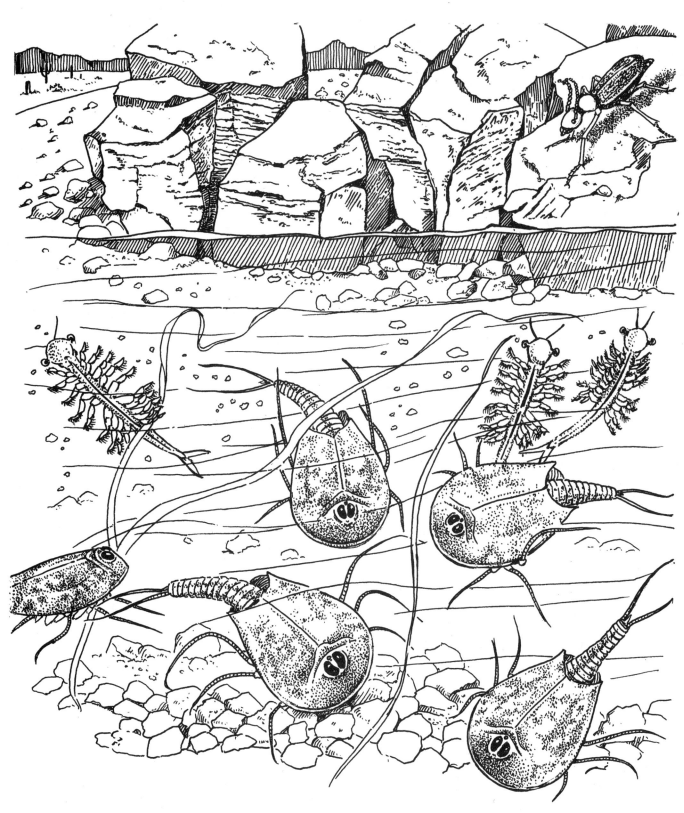

The temporary rainpool has enabled the hatching of tiny eggs that have lain dormant in the sand since last year's rains, and suddenly some primitive crustaceans appear in the pool: One is the **tadpole shrimp** (*Triops longicaudatus* or *Lepidurus* spp.), which looks like a tiny yellowish-brown horseshoe crab and whose fossil remains have been discovered in Triassic period deposits. The other is the **fairy shrimp** (*Brachinecta* spp.), a delicate transparent creature (with reddish touches) that swims on its back and feeds on one-celled algae after filtering them through the fine hairs on its legs. These creatures go through the complete life cycle of birth, reproduction, and death within ten days before the desert sun dries up the pool. When the pool dries up, a new cycle will begin. The microscopic eggs of these minute animals will lie in the sand undisturbed until the next season's heavy rainfall forms new pools.

A full century may go by before the slow-growing **giant saguaro** (*Carnegiea gigantea*) becomes treelike in appearance. Its arms, whose tips will bear white-petaled flowers with yellow centers, do not begin to grow before 15 to 30 years have passed. Desert birds such as Gila woodpeckers, elf owls, flickers, and cactus wrens find well-protected lodging in the saguaro. The 2-inch spines are a deterrent to most predators, except perhaps snakes. The saguaro's flowers bloom at night and are pollinated by nectar-sipping bats, insects, and—in the morning before the flowers close—birds such as the pale gray **white-winged dove** (*Zenaida asiatica*), which is seen here probing among the flowers. A male **Gila woodpecker** (*Melanerpes uropygialis*)—who sports a tannish-pink body, black-and-white barred wings, and a red spot on his head—can be seen bringing a tasty lizard to his mate in a nesting hole near the top of the saguaro.

At the very base of a **prickly pear cactus** (*Opuntia* spp.), one will sometimes find a large, well-protected nest made of cactus spines surrounding an inner sanctum of soft grasses. This is the home of the **white-throated woodrat** or **packrat** (*Neotoma albigula*)—which is about the size of a city rat, but somehow seems much cuter and cleaner. The life of the woodrat is always at risk, particularly at night when it leaves its prickly home to go foraging for

seeds, cactus, and other plants. Foxes, owls, and other predators are ever alert for such a tasty morsel. But most of the night prowlers dare not enter the spiny entranceways, for they are strewn with cactus needles and the prickly joints of the prickly pear's close relative, the **cholla** (also *Opuntia* spp.). How this rodent manages to escape injury in his own domain remains a mystery, but he seems quite content with his little home.

Against a background of crisp, white, yellow-centered **Mojave desert stars** (*Monoptilon bellioides*), the cylindrical **fishhook cactus** (*Mammillaria* spp. or *Sclerocactus* spp.) stands crowned by red-violet blooms circling its top. This cactus, which flowers from April through June, is unusual for its recurved or hooked spines. In the cactus's shade rests a **Gila monster** (*Heloderma suspectum*), which may grow to be 2 feet in length and is one of only two poisonous

lizards in the world. (The other is its even larger Mexican cousin, the beaded lizard.) Its coloring and texture resemble Native American beadwork. Its feet, legs, and the darker parts of its body are brownish-black, while the lighter areas are orange-buff to salmon pink.

The Gila monster is protected in Arizona. Though poisonous, it is hard to provoke, and has not been known to have caused any fatalities in healthy adults.

Before midday, when the heat (which can reach 150 degrees at ground level) becomes unbearable to most animals, the female **coyote** (*Canis latrans*) still hunts for food to bring home to her hungry pups. She has a gray coat with reddish undertones, a pale tan underside, yellowish-rust legs, and a black-tipped tail. Spotting a young **desert kangaroo rat** (*Dipodomys deserti*) still feeding, she pounces . . . and misses. Sensing danger, its gold-buff body, white undersides, and long white-tipped tail suddenly at attention, the kangaroo rat is gone in a flash, bounding almost 14 feet towards its burrow in one leap on its oversized hind legs.

The burrow, nest, and storehouse lie beneath a hillock and provide a sanctuary with many entrances and exits. Once below ground, the kangaroo rat is relatively safe from most predators except diggers such as the badger and kit fox.

On the edge of summer, in June, the coyote pups are about ten weeks old. These three have discovered a **regal horned lizard** (*Phrynosoma solare*) busily depleting an anthill not far from their den. Although they have been eating meat for the past three weeks, their curiosity about the horned lizard has overcome any desire to kill it. Their mother, watching their antics from above the rocky den, is tired after a long night's hunting and will soon, as the sun reaches its zenith, bed down under a rocky ledge nearby

to sleep away the rest of the day. The pups too will seek the cooler comfort of their den, abandoning play, the horned lizard, and the heat of midday.

The color of the coyote pups at ten weeks is a tawny yellow. The black tip on their tails has not yet developed, but a few black hairs are beginning to appear. The regal horned lizard is a pale brown; its head is slightly pinker in tone.

In the fierce midday heat, a **cactus wren** (*Campylorhynchus brunneicapillum*) searches for insects. Notice her prominent white eyestripe, rust-brown head, light-brown body with white stripes on the back, black-spotted white underbelly running to pale rust, and dark-brown-and-white spotted tail and wings. Her feather-lined nest in the cholla cactus in the left background is well protected against most predators except the black racer, a snake whose diet consists of bird's eggs and young nestlings.

In the middle distance a **kit fox** (*Vulpes macrotis*) is carrying a freshly killed **ground squirrel** (*Citellus* spp.) to her dugout, where she will hole up till darkness falls. Her coat is grayish buff, paler underneath and on its sides.

During periods of drought the long stalks of the **ocotillo** (*Fouquieria splendens*) in the right foreground shed their leaves and appear totally lifeless. But a good rain will bring forth new leaves and bell-shaped red flowers in clusters at the tips of each stalk.

A pale brown bird about the size of a robin, with darker streaks on its breast and neck and pale yellow eyes, sits on the branch of a flowering pink **tamarisk** or **saltcedar** (*Tamarix* spp.), singing with the sweet, melodious, crystal-clear warble that renders **Bendire's thrasher** (*Toxostoma bendirei*) one of the desert's most cherished songsters.

Above him, the saguaro awaits the returning **elf owl** (*Micrathene whitneyi*), America's tiniest owl. He has completed his nighttime search for food and is preparing to spend the searing daylight hours in his nesting hole. An endearing creature the size of a sparrow, the elf owl has large deep-yellow eyes crested with white and a brown body striped longitudinally with pale buff. He has a taste for large insects and is chiefly a nocturnal hunter. In fall, when the insects grow scarce, he will fly south to Mexico for the winter.

The butterfly at top right, with black-rimmed blue wings, is an **Antillean blue** (*Hemiargus ceraunus*).

Under the tamarisk's long clusters of pink flowers, the large black shining eyes of the **white-tailed antelope squirrel** (*Ammospermophilus leucurus*) watch for danger while he nibbles on seeds. This charming beast, who has a brownish-rust coat with white underside and a narrow white stripe running from tail to shoulder, looks much like a chipmunk. His black-edged tail is held over his back as he darts about, exposing its fluffy white underside. He lives in a burrow he has dug himself, but may also borrow an abandoned one or hole up in a crevice in a rocky ledge.

The **Coulter's lupine** (*Lupinus sparsiflorus*; also called **desert lupine**) in the foreground is a wonderful example of the beautiful flowers that can carpet the desert floor after a good rain. This lupine is either a bluish purple or a soft blue with a white upper petal. The small butterfly attracted to these flowers is a **Chara checkerspot** (*Dymasia chara*), which is yellow-orange with black trim.

After being caught in the thunderstorm of the night before, the **hognosed skunk** (*Conepatus leuconotus*), who is black beneath and has a white topside and tail, finally heads for his cool den in a crevice of an outcropping. Though his hunting habits are generally nocturnal, he still roots around for anything that might suit his appetite: insects, spiders, lizards, or small rodents.

A **horned owl** (*Bubo virginianus*), which is the skunk's only predator, watches sleepily from a nest of sticks and other bits of vegetation high in the crotch of a saguaro. But after the night's hunt his stomach is full of mice and a rabbit or two, and his interest is merely a matter of curiosity rather than hunger. This owl is quite large, up to 25 inches in length, and has hornlike ear tufts. His body is brownish gray on off-white and is striped horizontally with dark gray.

Rain in the desert will suddenly clothe what was once a barren landscape with a rainbow of wildflowers. In the right foreground is a **desert four o'clock** (*Mirabilis multiflora*), whose vivid pink flowers open in the evening. To the left, the large stand of prickly pear stretching toward a rocky abutment is medium green in color, studded with yellow flowers with pale yellow centers. Munching on the cactus is a large **desert tortoise** (*Gopherus agassizii*), about a foot long, with a thick, gray-brown shell and heavily scaled legs. When danger threatens, the tortoise withdraws into its shell and is protected from most predators (except man)—which helps it to live as long as fifty or sixty years.

Trying to keep cool in a deep cavity in the jumble of tannish rocks at the right is a large lizard (up to 16 inches long), the **chuckwalla** (*Sauromalus obesus*), black-headed, with a chubby, reddish-brown body.

An evergreen shrub with yellow-green leaves and pretty yellow flowers is one of the most common shrubs of the desert. The **creosote bush** (*Larrea tridentata*) endures very high temperatures, will grow where other plants cannot, and will flower three or four times in a season. It produces a pungent odor much like the preservative, creosote; though not many animals care to nibble its foliage it does play host to mantids, crickets, and grasshoppers.

It is midday now, and this **black-tailed jackrabbit** (*Lepus californicus*) is resting in the form he has dug in the shadow of the creosote. His large ears help to disperse his body heat. His fur is light gray and black, with a white underside and a short tail that is striped black above and edged with white.

Trailing along the sand in the foreground is a bad-smelling vine called the **buffalo gourd** (*Cucurbita foetidissima*), whose flowers are medium yellow and whose inedible fruit is sometimes dried and painted in bright colors.

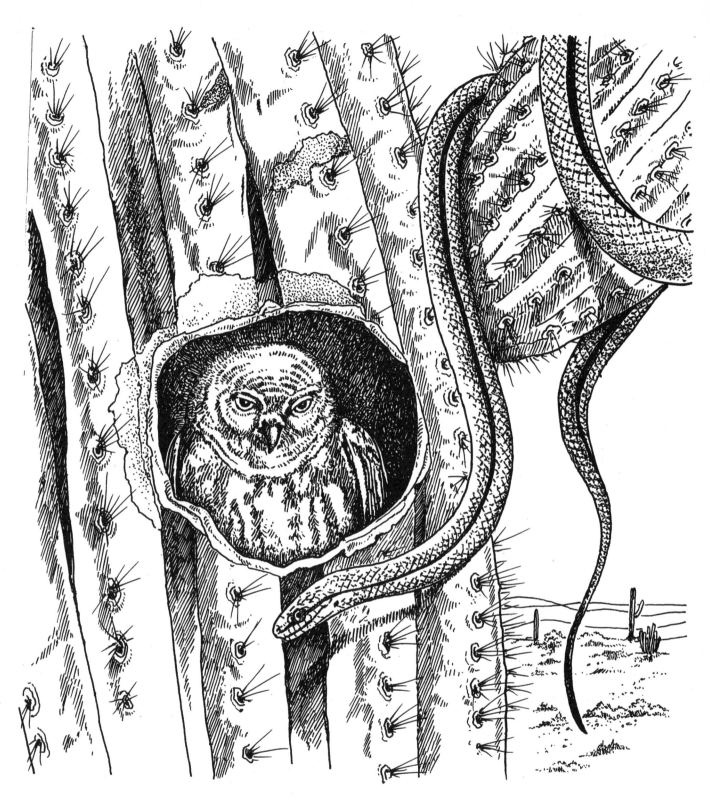

The noontime sun has become intense, the air is still, and only the shrill cry of the Gila woodpecker occasionally breaks the silence. The hunters and the hunted alike are already bedded down either in their cooler underground nests or under some shady shrub to sleep away the daylight hours. But predators such as the **Sonoran whipsnake** (*Masticophis bilineatus*) are diurnal and are forever on the prowl. This snake is hungry and on the lookout for nestlings or lizards, neither of which he will find in this saguaro. He is long and slender, olive-brown or bluish gray above, with a narrow black stripe running from eye to tail. His underside is a buffy yellow tinged with pale orange.

The elf owl above him, fairly safe in the saguaro hole, is not exactly what the snake is looking for. This owl has settled down for a full day's sleep, but the cool of evening will bring him out again, and the tiny bird will wreak havoc on the nighttime insect population.

With long tough nails on his turned-in forefeet, short legs, and a body whose loose skin allows him to flatten into a newly dug hole, the **badger** (*Taxidea taxus*) is one of the fastest and most determined diggers in the animal kingdom. His beautiful long-haired coat is pale gray with hints of brown. He has black feet, a black face with a narrow white stripe running between his eyes to his back, a white chin and cheeks, and black-rimmed white ears.

His intended dinner, a kangaroo rat, was asleep when she felt the earth move. She scampered to an exit hole and now watches from a safe distance while the badger quickly digs down to her vacant nest and destroys it. Dismayed at the loss of his prey, the badger finally will give up the cause and waddle off. The kangaroo rat will run back home to repair the damage. After a while, having made a few trembling trips topside for fresh soft grass to line her nest, she will sleep again, this time unhampered.

One of the important members on the desert's ecological roll call is a blackish-brown bird about 32 inches long with a huge wingspread of nearly 6 feet. The **turkey vulture** (*Cathartes aura*), which is found in most of the United States, has a naked reddish head and light yellow feet. Its flight feathers are spread like fingers as it flies and are a slightly lighter shade of blackish brown. Many of these birds can be seen soaring on updrafts above the desert country, searching endlessly for dead or dying animals. Their remarkable sense of smell and uncanny eyesight help make them an invaluable part of nature's cleanup squad.

The yellow-flowered **century plant** (*Agave americana*), despite its name, usually lives only ten to twenty-five years. It flowers only once in its lifetime, and then dies. The flowering stalk may grow to 40 feet in height. The thick, drab green leaves are sharply pointed and have cruel spines along their edges.

As the temperature climbs higher and higher the coyote will look to his favorite spot under the **smoketree** (*Psorothamnus spinosus*). Like the other members of the dog family, coyotes have the ability to cool themselves by panting. Some of the smaller creatures of the desert must seek underground burrows in order to deal with excessive body heat. The coyote will sleep away the hottest hours of this summer day and will awake when the sun begins to dip below the horizon and the sky turns a fiery pink.

Hunger will once more drive him to hunt; kangaroo rats, mice, even lizards—anything that moves will be part of his menu tonight.

The smoketree is loaded with fragrant, purple flowers, and provides him a densely shaded hideaway day after day. Smoketrees are leafless most of the year; the leaves that appear in the spring fall off before the flowers bloom. The tree's many twigs are hairy, smoky gray, and spiny.

Midafternoon heat finds most of the small desert creatures asleep in their underground nests or below the layer of litter on the surface—except for the jackrabbits, which seem to find the shade of shrubs or rock cool enough for comfort. Larger animals such as coyotes or bobcats prefer to wait out the blistering heat in whatever shade is available; and though the high temperatures can be fatal to birds, they too find roosts in the open or in trees or shrubbery. Snakes and lizards, though they need some

warmth to exist, would certainly perish in the desert's 120 to 150 degrees, so by and large they also seek the cool shade of rocky outcrops or ledges. Or, as the horned lizard or **sidewinder rattlesnake** (*Crotalus cerastes*) do, they may dig beneath the sand's shallow surface to stay out of the sun's scorching rays.

Even in a nest or burrow deep below ground, the animals' internal clocks waken them at twilight to take up their nighttime activities again.

As the moon rises at twilight, cooler breezes sweep in from the low mountains to wash away some of the unbearable daytime heat, and animals large and small are beginning to stir. At the rainpool, which has grown noticeably smaller, the coyote will satisfy his thirst, but not before a **desert cottontail** (*Sylvilagus auduboni*) has fled in a panic. Overhead, with a soft, high-pitched cry and an even softer flutter of wings, the elf owl leaves his nesting hole in the saguaro in the never-ending search for food.

Off in the brush one can hear the clucking of a group of Gambel's quail along with a soft grunting which means the peccaries are abroad again, probably heading for the pool. Silhouetted against the sky, the **bobcat** (*Lynx rufus*) stands, fully awake, hungry, and scanning his domain. Pretty soon it will be dark, and with the darkness the eternal business of predators and prey will once again commence.

The great horned owl, after hunting in the dark on silent wings, sits quietly on a branch of a **yellow palo verde** (*Cercidium microphyllum*) tree, against a lemon-yellow moon. One of the grand predators at the top of the food chain, the owl lives on rodents such as this white-tailed antelope squirrel. Though the squirrel is dead, life goes on, following the great circle of the food chain. The sun's energy goes first into plants and then is passed along to the rodents and insects that feed on plants; then it goes to the smaller predators that feed on rodents and insects, and on to the larger predators such as owls, badgers, pumas, and bobcats, that feed on the smaller predators. When death takes any animal or plant, the remains decay and are returned to the soil, to be broken down as ammonia and other nitrogen compounds—exactly what plants néed to grow. And so the chain is complete, and every plant and animal has contributed to the continuum of life on this planet we call home.

This **tiger rattlesnake** (*Crotalus tigris*) has suddenly sensed the presence of a possible meal. The snake needn't actually see its prey. A small pit located between its nostrils and its eyes contains nerves that help it to locate prey by their body heat. The rattler glides to within two feet of a **silky pocket mouse** (*Perognathus flavus*) digging furiously to restore its underground burrow, which was destroyed earlier by a hungry kit fox. The little mouse nearly overlooks the snake's stealthy approach—but at the last moment it pops into a runway to its old nest. Frustrated momentarily, the rattler slithers by, testing the air for new prey.

The tiger rattlesnake, which is smaller than most other rattlers, is a pale buffy tan in color, with darker tan bands. The silky pocket mouse has a white underside and chin and is light yellowish brown above with some black hairs. It has a yellowish patch behind its ear and a white patch beneath the ear.

Because of its spectacular flowers, people have taken many specimens of the **night-blooming cereus** (*Peniocereus greggii*) from its natural habitat and sold them for use in gardens. The federal government has tried to prevent this sort of depredation by listing this cactus as a "sensitive" species. The night-blooming cereus is thin, twiglike, and sparsely spined. It grows beneath other desert plants, such as the creosote bush, and when it is not flowering it looks like a dead branch. During periods of drought it will call upon the water it has stored in its large tuberous roots, which may weigh as much as 100 pounds. When this cactus blooms, its fragrant flowers—pure white, with pale yellow centers—attract the night-flying sphinx moths it relies on for its pollination. Usually all the night-blooming cereus plants in an area come into flower on the same night, filling the desert air with perfume. But when morning arrives, the flowers have already wilted.

A pretty little animal about the size of a house cat and weighing 3 to 6 pounds, the **kit fox** is a determined nocturnal hunter with a decided appetite for kangaroo rats. He spends the hot summer days below ground in a burrow he has dug or has commandeered from another animal and rises after dark to search for food. His enormous ears, attuned to the tiniest of sounds, are a great help in this search.

It is not easy for the fox to capture a kangaroo rat, which is able to make such magnificent leaps to safety. But the fox's speed and its digging abilities are enough to provide him with a healthy diet of these little rodents. If kangaroo rats are particularly hard to come by, there are always lizards, insects, and a rabbit or two to satisfy his empty stomach. The kit fox has buffy yellow sides; a gray and buff back, head, and tail; large deep-golden eyes; and a black tail tip.

An unusual visitor has just arrived—a **red-spotted toad** (*Bufo punctatus*), who may have traveled as far as a mile to this rainpool, one of the few still left after the last downpour. Every so often he remembers to trill sweetly to announce his presence to any females in the area. But his desire for female companionship will be overcome temporarily by his appetite for any flying moth or other insect that crosses his vision. This toad's coloring is a medium olive-gray or brown with red warts. His black pupils are surrounded with deep gold.

A few feet away, drinking in the moonlit water, is a female hog-nosed skunk with her two young. Three months old and still curious and playful, they stray momentarily until, wary, their mother spots the dim outline of a bobcat crouched in the shadows of the creosote bush. Whether the big cat will be willing to tangle with the skunk family will depend on how hungry he is. Most animals wouldn't chance it!

The bobcat is about to learn a lesson he should have learned long ago. One of the hog-nosed skunk youngsters, still unacquainted with all the dangers of desert life, has followed a large beetle too close to the creosote bush. The crouching bobcat has decided to act—but just when he is about to pounce the air is filled with a pungency only an angry skunk can produce. The encounter is over in seconds; the cat rolls for a moment in the dust as if hoping to escape the odor and dashes into the darkness of the rocky ledges. The skunk, still shaking with rage, gathers her young and hustles them off to a safer feeding ground. The bobcat will spend the rest of the night cleaning, as best he can, his strong-smelling fur.

As the moon rises, a small group of **mule deer** (*Odocoileus hemionus*) have come down from the hills for a drink at the rainpool. Though they spend the majority of their lives in the forested regions above the desert, a moonlit night will bring them to the desert floor to forage for cactus fruit, yucca, and other savory plants. A gentle animal, quite fleet of foot, this deer has very large ears, somewhat like a mule's (hence the name), that flick independently of each other in all directions to pick up any sounds that might mean lurking danger. Mule deer do not have many enemies—but coyotes, bobcats, and the occasional puma are enough to make them very wary, especially if there are fawns about.

Summer finds the mule deer in a red-brown or yellow-brown coat, with white at the throat and rump and inside the ears and legs. The tail is white with a black tip.

There is a kind of music to the wilderness. Whether it is created by birds singing in an open woodland, the rush of wind through the treetops, the gentle ripple of water in a stream, or the lulling sounds of crickets in the tall grass at night—each ecology has its own diverse rhythms, its own songs. The desert, not to be outdone, has not only its beautiful morning birdcalls and the endless musical hum of insects during the heat of day, but also a master serenader.

When there is moonlight, and the coyote rests a bit from hunting, he sometimes rejoices with others of his kind. His howl, musical in every way, is slightly higher-pitched than that of a wolf and is punctuated by short barks and yips. It is a song of the vast open country he lives in—and as he howls to the stars, one cannot help but believe that he is at one with the environment he lives in and that his is a song of pure joy.

INDEX OF COMMON NAMES OF PLANTS AND ANIMALS

INDEX OF SCIENTIFIC NAMES OF PLANTS AND ANIMALS